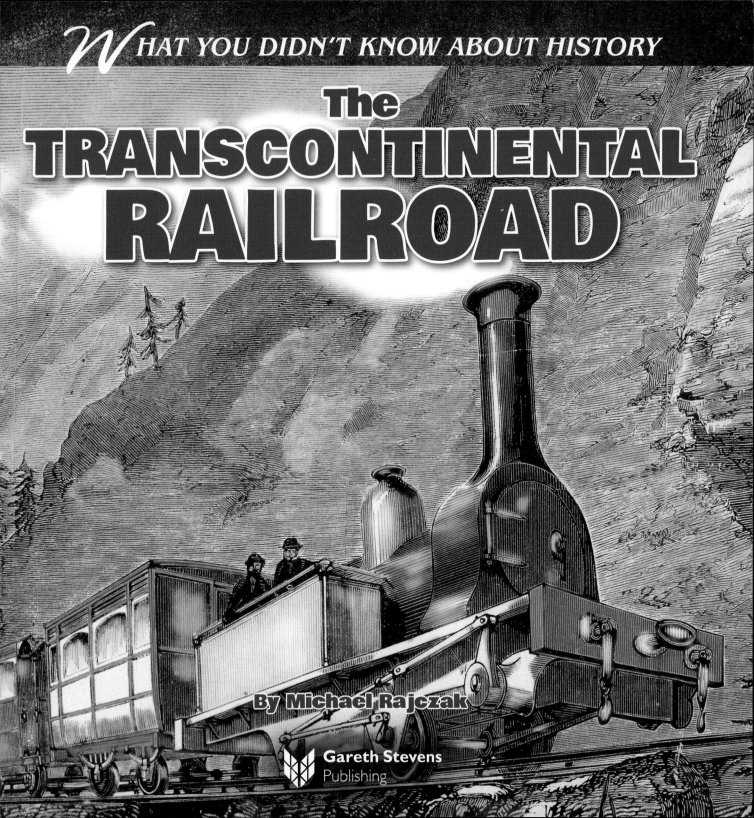

The TRANSCONTINENTAL RAILROAD

By Michael Rajczak

Gareth Stevens
Publishing

Please visit our website, www.garethstevens.com. For a free color catalog of all our high-quality books, call toll free 1-800-542-2595 or fax 1-877-542-2596.

Library of Congress Cataloging-in-Publication Data

Rajczak, Michael.
The Transcontinental Railroad / by Michael Rajczak.
  p. cm. — (What you didn't know about history)
Includes index.
ISBN 978-1-4824-0599-6(pbk.)
ISBN 978-1-4824-0597-2 (6-pack)
ISBN 978-1-4824-0600-9 (library binding)
1. Pacific railroads — Juvenile literature. 2. Railroads — History — Juvenile literature. I. Rajczak, Michael. II. Title.
TF25.P23 R35 2014
625.261—dc23

First Edition

Published in 2014 by
Gareth Stevens Publishing
111 East 14th Street, Suite 349
New York, NY 10003

Copyright © 2014 Gareth Stevens Publishing

Designer: Andrea Davison-Bartolotta
Editor: Kristen Rajczak

Photo credits: Cover, pp. 1, 16 Prisma/UIG/Getty Images; p. 4 Carelton Watkins/Wikimedia Commons; p. 5 Alexander Helser/FPG/Archive Photos/Getty Images; p. 7 (map) Seyyahil/Shutterstock.com; p. 7 (background) iStockphoto/Thinkstock; p. 8 Kean Collection/Archive Photos/Getty Images; p. 9 Archive Photos/Stringer/Getty Images; p. 11 (main) Underwood Archives/Getty Images; pp. 11 (inset), 17 MPI/Stringer/Getty Images; p. 13 Hulton Archive/Getty Images; p. 15 Interim Archives/Getty Images; p. 18 Dr_Flash/Shutterstock.com; p. 19 SuperStock/Getty Images; p. 20 Henry Guttmann/Stringer/Hulton Archive/Getty Images.

Interactive eBook credits: pp. 4–5, 10–11 MPI/Stringer/Getty Images; pp. 6–7 ApexStock/Image Bank Film/Getty Images; pp. 8–9 Fotosearch/Stringer/Getty Images; pp. 12–13 A. J. Russell/MPI/Getty Images; pp. 14–15 Universal History Archive/Getty Images; pp. 16–17 Dr_Flash/Shutterstock.com; pp. 18–19 Jerry Susoeff/Shutterstock.com; pp. 20–21 Doug Jensen/Shutterstock.com.

Printed in the United States of America

CPSIA compliance information: Batch #CW14GS: For further information contact Gareth Stevens, New York, New York at 1-800-542-2595.

CONTENTS

Crazy Theodore Judah 4

All the Way to the Pacific 6

The Chinese and the Irish 8

A Usual Day 10

During Off Hours 12

Blasting Through Solid Rock 14

Native American Land 16

Finally! 18

Impact 20

Glossary 22

For More Information 23

Index 24

Words in the glossary appear in **bold** type the first time they are used in the text.

CRAZY THEODORE JUDAH

Before the **American Civil War**, many people wondered if a railroad crossing the entire nation was possible. An **engineer** named Theodore Judah believed it could be done! Despite his finding a way for a **transcontinental** railroad to cross the huge Sierra Nevada mountain range, Judah's dream earned him the nickname "Crazy Judah."

By 1860, Judah already had some of the money needed to make the railroad happen. He asked Congress for help, and in 1862, the Pacific Railroad Act passed, allowing him to begin building his dream.

Theodore Judah

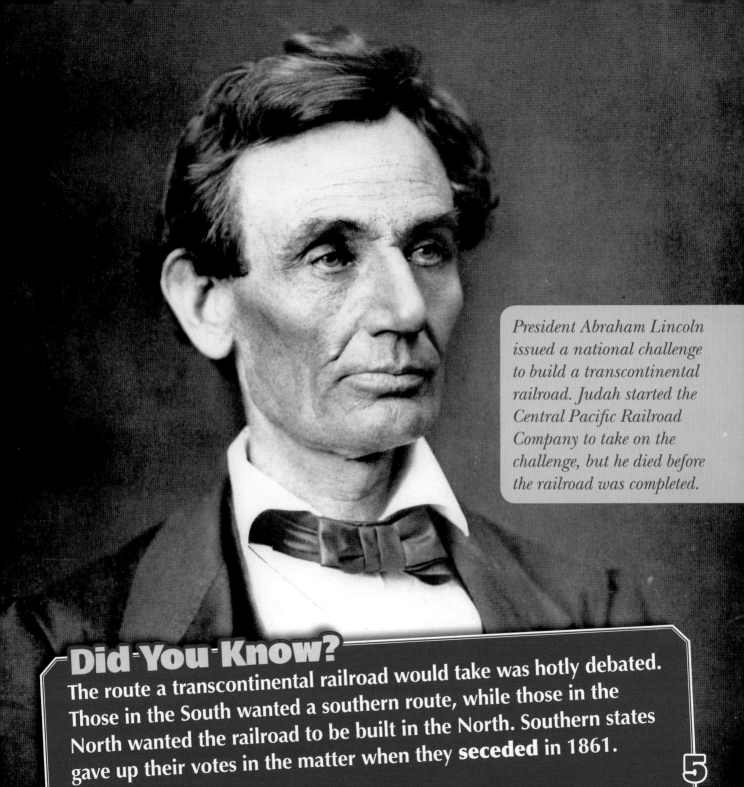

President Abraham Lincoln issued a national challenge to build a transcontinental railroad. Judah started the Central Pacific Railroad Company to take on the challenge, but he died before the railroad was completed.

Did You Know?

The route a transcontinental railroad would take was hotly debated. Those in the South wanted a southern route, while those in the North wanted the railroad to be built in the North. Southern states gave up their votes in the matter when they **seceded** in 1861.

ALL THE WAY TO THE PACIFIC

Gold and silver discoveries in California were drawing people west, so a transcontinental railroad made sense. But it was still a huge undertaking during the 1860s.

Two companies were hired to build the tracks. Theodore Judah's Central Pacific Railroad would build eastward from Sacramento, California, through the Sierra Nevada. The Union Pacific would work westward from Omaha, Nebraska, across the Great Plains and Rocky Mountains. Central Pacific started laying their track in 1863, and the race was on to see who could cross the most miles!

Did You Know?

The US government promised railroad companies land on both sides of the track. They were paid $16,000 for every mile of track they put down, more if the track was through hills and mountains.

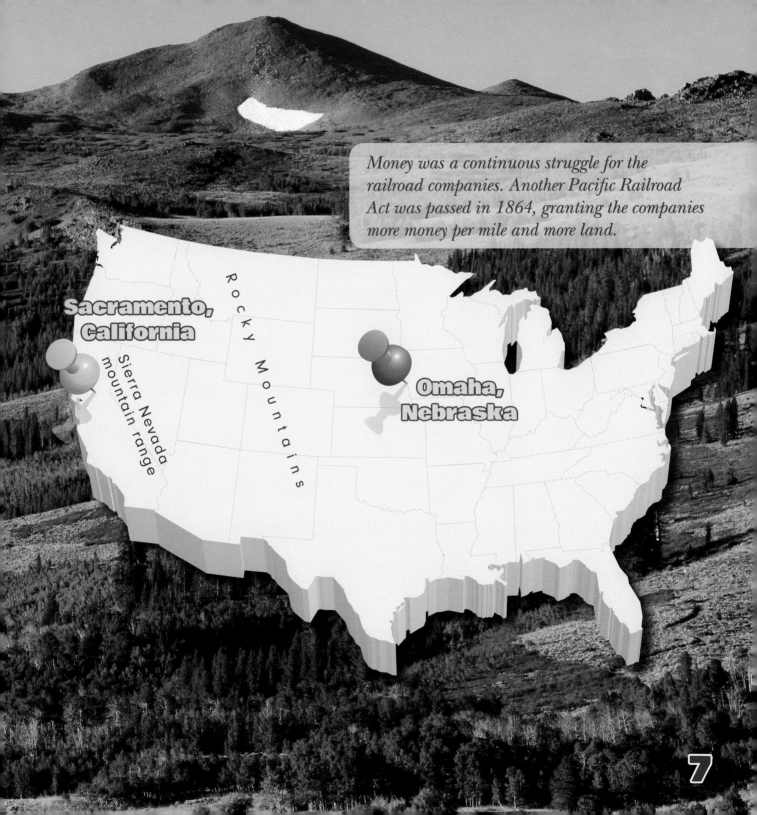

Money was a continuous struggle for the railroad companies. Another Pacific Railroad Act was passed in 1864, granting the companies more money per mile and more land.

Sacramento, California

Rocky Mountains

Sierra Nevada mountain range

Omaha, Nebraska

THE CHINESE AND THE IRISH

Building a railroad is backbreaking work. The Union Pacific hired many soldiers who had fought in the Civil War. Both companies also hired Irish **immigrants**. But the Central Pacific had a hard time keeping their workers. They began hiring Chinese immigrants and even **advertising** the railroad jobs in China.

Chinese workers were often treated badly. They were paid less and had to buy their own food, though the other workers had theirs provided. By 1866, 75 percent of the Central Pacific workers were Chinese!

Some Chinese immigrants came to the United States through agreements similar to those of indentured servants, which means their passage was paid for by a person or company and they had to work a certain number of years in order to pay the cost back.

Did You Know?

The Chinese came to work for Central Pacific partly because the Irish workers wanted more money. There also was a shortage of men willing to do the hard labor of building the railroad—especially when they might get rich looking for gold and silver instead!

9

A USUAL DAY

The lowly railroad workers were on the job for about 12 hours a day, 6 days a week. They labored through the summer heat. In the winter, they dug tunnels through giant snowdrifts to continue working.

The workers did the same thing every day. They used tools to level the land for the tracks. Heavy wooden ties and metal tracks were carried as far as possible by railcars. Then, the supplies were loaded onto horse-drawn flat cars that took them to the track's current end.

Did You Know?

If the tunnels under snowdrifts caved in, workers sometimes would have to wait until spring to get the bodies out. Thousands of workers were buried in shallow graves all along the transcontinental railroad.

The most productive day on the transcontinental railroad saw 10 miles (16 km) of track laid.

10 MILES OF TRACK, LAID IN ONE DAY. APRIL 28TH 1869

DURING OFF HOURS

After a long day working, Chinese workers would take warm sponge baths and change their clothing before eating dinner. They had their own cooks who prepared many different kinds of food: dried oysters, fish, rice, salted cabbage, and dried fruits. They also ate pork, poultry, mushrooms, and vegetables. That makes the beef, beans, and potatoes the Irish workers ate seem boring!

The Chinese workers liked playing fan-tan, a game in which players place bets on numbers on a board. They had their own Buddhist priests in their camps, too!

Did You Know?

Irish workers drank water while on the job, but Chinese workers drank weak tea made in the camp and brought in barrels to the work area. Since the tea water was boiled, it was cleaner than the water Irish workers drank, which sometimes made them sick.

Chinese and Irish railroad workers toiled in all sorts of weather. After, they went to their camps and usually slept in tents.

13

BLASTING THROUGH SOLID ROCK

Central Pacific's work slowed once they reached the Sierra Nevada. There was lots of ice and snow, and the workers needed to tunnel *through* the mountains! They drilled holes and filled them with nitroglycerine or black powder to blast through the rock.

After the explosion, workers cleared the **debris**. More holes were drilled, and the process would repeat for weeks at a time. Though powerful, nitroglycerine was also dangerous. Accidental explosions and the rock slides caused by tunneling killed as many as 1,500 Chinese workers.

Central Pacific's greatest **obstacle** was the Sierra Nevada. Because of this mountain range, they had to create more than three times as many tunnel miles as the Union Pacific.

Did You Know?

Rivers and canyons had to be crossed by the tracks as well. Strong **trestles** and bridges had to be built. More than 300 Chinese workers fell to their death during the year it took to build over the American River canyon.

NATIVE AMERICAN LAND

Of the more than 1,000 battles fought between white settlers and Native Americans, many were caused by the building of the transcontinental railroad. Native Americans on the plains relied on the herds of bison for food. Railroad companies believed the bison could cause problems for trains and began to kill them.

Native American attack on a Union Pacific train

Conflicts also happened because railroad workers cut down whole forests for wood for railroad ties. Other clashes were a result of the railroad route going through **sacred** Native American lands and hunting grounds.

Killing bison on the Great Plains hurt the Native American way of life—and they were angry about it!

The two rail companies finally met at Promontory Summit in Utah on May 10, 1869. The Central Pacific had laid 690 miles (1,110 km) of track, while the Union Pacific had put down 1,086 miles (1,747 km) of track.

Governor Leland Stanford of California, who had been president of the Central Pacific, had the honor of putting the last spike into place. Many accounts say the spike was made of gold, but others say it was only gold-plated since gold would be too soft to be driven into a railroad tie.

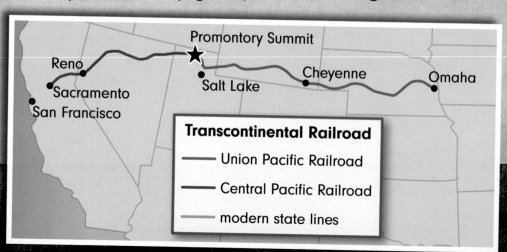

Promontory Summit

Reno

Sacramento

San Francisco

Salt Lake

Cheyenne

Omaha

Transcontinental Railroad

— Union Pacific Railroad

— Central Pacific Railroad

— modern state lines

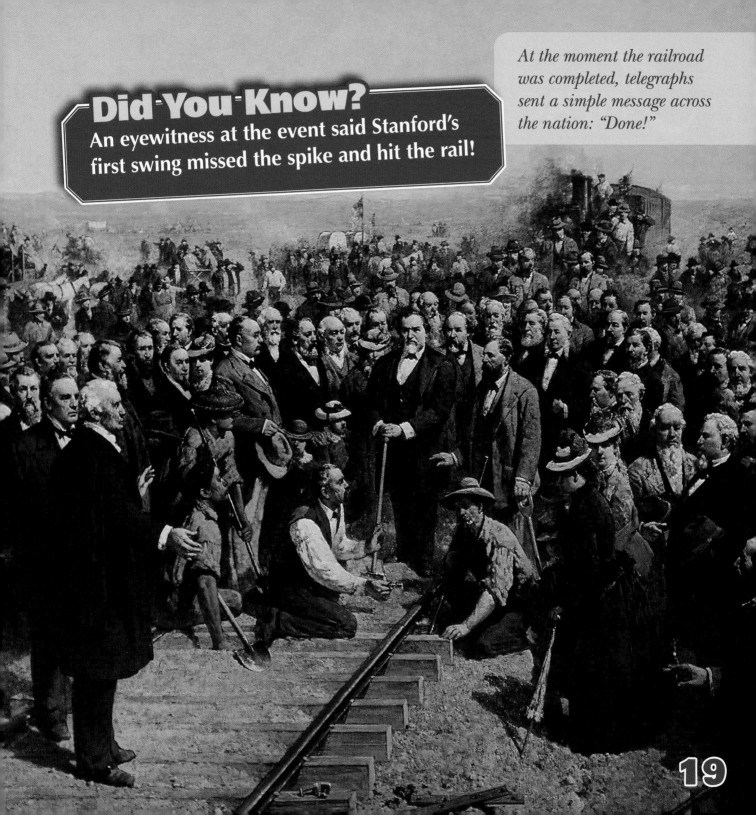

Did You Know?
An eyewitness at the event said Stanford's first swing missed the spike and hit the rail!

At the moment the railroad was completed, telegraphs sent a simple message across the nation: "Done!"

Using the transcontinental railroad, traveling between New York City and San Francisco, California, might take as little as a week! The cost for a passenger became affordable, about $65 to $100. The cost of shipping dropped, too. This improved manufacturing and movement of goods.

However, the thousands of railroad workers had no jobs. Dislike of the Chinese made it doubly hard for these immigrants to make a living. In addition, the near **extinction** of the bison forever changed the Native American way of life on the plains.

Did You Know?

The 1869 meeting of the two rail lines didn't actually connect the two coasts! It wasn't until the following year that a person could travel across the whole country by rail.

Along the Transcontinental Railroad

November 1860	Theodore Judah and several businessmen form the Central Pacific Railroad Company.
July 1, 1862	The Pacific Railroad Act passes, allowing the Central Pacific to build a railroad starting in California and hiring the Union Pacific Railroad Company to build westward.
October 26, 1863	Central Pacific "spikes" its first rails to ties.
January 1865	The first Chinese workers are hired by Central Pacific.
July 10, 1865	Union Pacific "spikes" its first rails.
April 28, 1869	Central Pacific workers lay 10 miles (16 km) of rail in 1 day!
May 10, 1869	The railroads of Central Pacific and Union Pacific meet.

GLOSSARY

advertise: to make publicly known, especially by a printed notice

American Civil War: a war fought from 1861 to 1865 in the United States between the Union (the Northern states) and the Confederacy (the Southern states)

debris: the remains of something that has been broken

engineer: someone who plans and builds machines

extinction: the death of all members of a species

immigrant: one who comes to a new country to settle there

obstacle: something that blocks a path

sacred: specially blessed

secede: to leave a country

transcontinental: extending across a continent

trestle: a framework of wood and metal that holds up a road or railroad over a low point in the land

FOR MORE INFORMATION

Books

Orr, Tamra. *The Railroad and the Civil War (1860s)*. Hockessin, DE: Mitchell Lane Publishers, 2013.

Stein, R. Conrad. *The Incredible Transcontinental Railroad*. Berkeley Heights, NJ: Enslow Publishers, 2012.

Websites

Transcontinental Railroad
www.history.com/topics/transcontinental-railroad
Read more about the building of the transcontinental railroad and other topics during that time period.

Westward Expansion: First Transcontinental Railroad
www.ducksters.com/history/westward_expansion/ first_transcontinental_railroad.php
Learn fun facts about the transcontinental railroad and some of the other interesting events of westward expansion in the United States.

Index

American Civil War 4, 8

bison 16, 17, 20

bridges 15

Central Pacific Railroad 5, 6, 8, 9, 14, 15, 18, 21

Chinese 8, 9, 12, 13, 14, 15, 20, 21

deaths 10, 14, 15

food 12, 16

gold spike 18

Great Plains 6, 16, 17, 20

Irish 8, 9, 12, 13

Judah, Theodore 4, 5, 6, 21

Lincoln, Abraham 5

Native Americans 16, 17, 20

Omaha, Nebraska 6

Pacific Railroad Act 4, 7, 21

Pawnee tribe 17

Promontory Summit, Utah 18

Rocky Mountains 6

Sacramento, California 6

Sierra Nevada 4, 6, 14, 15

Stanford, Leland 18, 19

trestles 15

tunnels 14, 15

Union Pacific Railroad 6, 8, 15, 16, 17, 18, 21

water 13

workday 10